Holy Bible

INTERNATIONAL CHILDREN'S BIBLE

THE GOSPEL OF MARK

NEW CENTURY VERSION

Holy Bible

INTERNATIONAL CHILDREN'S BIBLE

THE GOSPEL OF MARK

Authentic

INTERNATIONAL CHILDREN'S BIBLE - THE GOSPEL OF MARK
New Century Version

29 28 27 26 25 24 23   8 7 6 5 4 3 2

BRITISH LIBRARY CATALOGUING IN PUBLISHING DATA
A catalogue record for this book is available from the British Library.

ISBN: 978-1-78893-146-5

Published by Authentic Media,
PO Box 6326, Bletchley, Milton Keynes, MK1 9GG United Kingdom. All rights reserved.
First produced by Bookprint Creative Services.
Printed and bound by Micropress Printers Ltd, Suffolk, IP18 6SZ, UK.

Holy Bible

INTERNATIONAL CHILDREN'S BIBLE

THE GOSPEL OF MARK

PRESENTED TO . . .

. . . .

FROM . . . Littleport Churches Together

DATE . . . 16th August 2024

WHAT IS THE BIBLE?

The Bible is God's holy Word, which he has spoken to help us to find out more about himself, and the life he wants us to lead. The Bible is made up of 66 books, from Genesis through to Revelation. These books have an incredible way of fitting together to form a whole. Each book is special on its own, but put together, all these books give us the history of what God has done in our world and his message of love and hope through his Son, Jesus Christ who came to live, to die, and to save us.

The Bible is not just a book of amazing stories but also a personal guide for us to follow. God has not left us to struggle on our own; instead he has purposefully used history, writing, culture and people to talk to us. Inside is adventure, excitement, battles and mysteries. There is, though, some serious reading and learning – God is the authority and his Word should not ever be distorted, ignored or added to. There are no mistakes in what God has said, and we now have the chance to discover the Truth. The Holy Bible is a reliable book and worth reading all the way through! (More than once!)

This Bible was especially translated for children to read and understand.

There are two major sections of the Bible: the *Old Testament* and the *New Testament*. This edition contains only the Gospel of Mark from the *New Testament*.

There are 39 books in the *Old Testament*, mostly written by Jews, in their own language, Hebrew. It begins with the story of how God created the world, the sky, the earth, the animals, the trees and human beings in his image and proved his goodness to us through creation. The history continues through God's special people, the Jews. We learn about prophets and what God has told them to tell us. They spoke a lot about a very special person, the Messiah. It really is quite surprising as to how accurate they were, and it is proof that God really told them what was to come in the future.

The *New Testament* has 27 books, written by Christians, mostly in Greek, which was the language they spoke. This second section starts with the birth of Jesus Christ, God's son. It tells us what Jesus said, how He was killed and then came back to life again. It also explains that one day He will come back. This testament tells us how Jesus' teaching led to the start and continued growth of the Christian church and how to continue within that today.

Everyone who has heard or reads the Gospel must either: accept Jesus and receive his power, or leave him behind. Who is Jesus to you? A name or a friend? If as yet you don't know, at least read and reply to the agreement below.

I ....

promise to read and try to understand that the Bible is from God. If I find that this book tells me the truth and that Jesus Christ is my Saviour and Lord, I will accept him and try to follow him my whole life.

(Signed) ....

(Dated) ....

MARK

Mark Tells About the Power of Jesus

John Prepares for Jesus

1 This is the beginning of the Good News[d] about Jesus Christ, the Son of God,[n] 2 as the prophet[d] Isaiah wrote:

"I will send my messenger ahead
of you.
He will prepare your way."
Malachi 3:1

3 "There is a voice of a man who calls out in the desert:
'Prepare the way for the Lord.
Make the road straight for
him'." *Isaiah 40:3*

4 John was baptising people in the desert. He preached a baptism of changed hearts and lives for the forgiveness of sins. 5 All the people from Judea and Jerusalem were going out to John. They told about the sins they had done. Then they were baptised by him in the Jordan River. 6 John wore clothes made from camel's hair and had a leather belt around his waist. He ate locusts[d] and wild honey. 7 This is what John preached to the people: "There is one coming later who is greater than I. I am not good enough even to kneel down and untie his sandals. 8 I baptise you with water. But the one who is coming will baptise you with the Holy Spirit."[d]

Jesus Is Baptised

9 At that time Jesus came from the town of Nazareth in Galilee to the place where John was. John baptised Jesus in the Jordan River. 10 When Jesus was coming up out of the water, he saw heaven open. The Holy Spirit[d] came down on him like a dove. 11 A voice came from heaven and said: "You are my Son and I love you. I am very pleased with you."

12 Then the Spirit sent Jesus into the desert alone. 13 He was in the desert 40 days and was there with the wild animals. While he was in the desert, he was tempted by Satan. Then angels came and took care of Jesus.

Jesus Chooses Some Followers

14 After John was put in prison, Jesus went into Galilee and preached the Good News[d] from God. 15 Jesus said, "The right time has come. The kingdom of God is near. Change your hearts and lives and believe the Good News!"

16 When Jesus was walking by Lake Galilee, he saw Simon[n] and Simon's brother, Andrew. They were fishermen and were throwing a net into the lake to catch fish. 17 Jesus said to them, "Come and follow me. I will make you fishermen for men." 18 So Simon and Andrew immediately left their nets and followed him.

19 Jesus continued walking by Lake Galilee. He saw two more brothers, James and John, the sons of Zebedee. They were in their boat, preparing their nets to catch fish. 20 Their father Zebedee and the men who worked for him were in the boat with the brothers. When Jesus saw the brothers, he called them to come with

him. They left their father and followed Jesus.

Jesus Removes an Evil Spirit

21 Jesus and his followers went to Capernaum. On the Sabbath*d* day Jesus went to the synagogue*d* and began to teach. 22 The people there were amazed at his teaching. He did not teach like their teachers of the law. He taught like a person who had authority. 23 While he was in the synagogue, a man was there who had an evil spirit in him. The man shouted, 24 "Jesus of Nazareth! What do you want with us? Did you come to destroy us? I know who you are – God's Holy One!" 25 Jesus said strongly, "Be quiet! Come out of the man!" 26 The evil spirit made the man shake violently. Then the spirit gave a loud cry and came out of him. 27 The people were amazed. They asked each other, "What is happening here? This man is teaching something new. And he teaches with authority. He even gives commands to evil spirits, and they obey him." 28 And the news about Jesus spread quickly everywhere in the area of Galilee.

Jesus Heals Many People

29 Jesus and his followers left the synagogue.*d* They all went at once with James and John to the home of Simon*n* and Andrew. 30 Simon's mother-in-law was sick in bed with a fever. The people there told Jesus about her. 31 So Jesus went to her bed, took her hand, and helped her up. Immediately the fever left her, and she was healed. Then she began serving them.

32 That night, after the sun went down, the people brought to Jesus all who were sick. They also brought those who had demons*d* in them. 33 The whole town gathered at the door of the house. 34 Jesus healed many who had different kinds of sickness. He also forced many demons to leave people. But he would not allow the demons to speak, because they knew who he was.

35 Early the next morning, Jesus woke and left the house while it was still dark. He went to a place to be alone and pray. 36 Later, Simon and his friends went to look for Jesus. 37 They found him and said, "Everyone is looking for you!"

38 Jesus answered, "We should go somewhere else, to other towns around here. Then I can preach there too. That is the reason I came." 39 So he travelled everywhere in Galilee. He preached in the synagogues and forced demons to leave people.

Jesus Heals a Sick Man

40 A man who had a harmful skin disease came to Jesus. The man fell to his knees and begged Jesus, "I know that you can heal me if you will."

41 Jesus felt sorry for the man. So he touched him and said, "I want to heal you. Be healed!" 42 At once the disease left the man, and he was healed.

43 Jesus told the man to go at once. But Jesus warned him strongly, 44 "Don't tell anyone about what I did for you, but go and show yourself to the priest. And offer a gift to God because you have been healed. Offer the gift that Moses commanded.*n* This will show the people that you are healed." 45 The man left there, but he told everyone he saw that Jesus had healed him. So the news about Jesus

Simon Simon's other name was Peter.
Moses commanded Read about this in Leviticus 14:1–32.

spread. That is the reason Jesus could not enter a town if people saw him. He stayed in places where nobody lived. But people came from all the towns to wherever he was.

Jesus Heals a Paralysed Man

2 A few days later, Jesus came back to Capernaum. The news spread that he was home. ²So many people gathered to hear him preach that the house was full. There was nowhere to stand, not even outside the door. Jesus was teaching them. ³Some people came, bringing a paralysed man to Jesus. Four of them were carrying the paralysed man. ⁴But they could not get to Jesus because of the crowd. So they went to the roof above Jesus and made a hole in the roof. Then they lowered the mat with the paralysed man on it. ⁵Jesus saw that these men had great faith. So he said to the paralysed man, "Young man, your sins are forgiven."

⁶Some of the teachers of the law were sitting there. They saw what Jesus did, and they said to themselves, ⁷"Why does this man say things like that? He is saying things that are against God. Only God can forgive sins."

⁸At once Jesus knew what these teachers of the law were thinking. So he said to them, "Why are you thinking these things? ⁹Which is easier: to tell this paralysed man, 'Your sins are forgiven', or to tell him, 'Stand up. Take your mat and walk'? ¹⁰But I will prove to you that the Son of Man*d* has authority on earth to forgive sins." So Jesus said to the paralysed man, ¹¹"I tell you, stand up. Take your mat and go home." ¹²Immediately the paralysed man stood up. He took his mat and walked out while everyone was watching him.

The people were amazed and

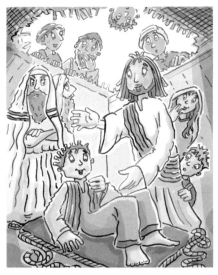

Mark 2:5 "Young man, your sins are forgiven."

praised God. They said, "We have never seen anything like this!"

¹³Jesus went to the lake again. A crowd followed him there, and he taught them. ¹⁴While he was walking beside the lake, he saw a tax collector named Levi son of Alphaeus. Levi was sitting in the tax office. Jesus said to him, "Follow me". And Levi stood up and followed Jesus.

¹⁵Later that day, Jesus ate at Levi's house. There were many tax collectors and "sinners" eating there with Jesus and his followers. Many people like this followed Jesus. ¹⁶The teachers of the law who were Pharisees*d* saw Jesus eating with the tax collectors and "sinners". They asked his followers, "Why does he eat with tax collectors and 'sinners'?"

¹⁷Jesus heard this and said to them, "Healthy people don't need a doctor. It is the sick who need a doctor. I did not come to invite good people. I came to invite sinners."

Jesus' Followers Are Criticised

[18] One day the followers of John[n] and the Pharisees[d] were giving up eating.[n] Some people came to Jesus and said, "John's followers and the followers of the Pharisees give up eating, but your followers don't. Why?"

[19] Jesus answered, "When there is a wedding, the friends of the bridegroom are not sad while he is with them. They do not give up eating while the bridegroom is still there. [20] But the time will come when the bridegroom will leave them. Then the friends will be sad and will give up eating.

[21] "When a person sews a patch over a hole on an old coat, he never uses a piece of cloth that is not yet shrunk. If he does, the patch will shrink and pull away from the coat. Then the hole will be worse. [22] Also, no one ever pours new wine into old leather bags for holding wine. If he does, the new wine will break the bags, and the wine will be ruined along with the bags for the wine. People always put new wine into new leather bags."

Jesus Is Lord of the Sabbath

[23] On the Sabbath[d] day, Jesus was walking through some grainfields. His followers were with him and picked some grain to eat. [24] The Pharisees[d] saw this and said to Jesus, "Why are your followers doing what is not lawful on the Sabbath?"

[25] Jesus answered, "You have read what David did when he and those with him were hungry and needed food. [26] It was during the time of Abiathar the high priest. David went into God's house and ate the bread that was made holy for God. The law of Moses says that only priests may eat that bread. But David also gave some of the bread to those who were with him."

[27] Then Jesus said to the Pharisees, "The Sabbath day was made to help people. They were not made to be ruled by the Sabbath day. [28] The Son of Man[d] is Lord even of the Sabbath."

Jesus Heals a Man's Crippled Hand

3 Another time when Jesus went into a synagogue,[d] a man with a crippled hand was there. [2] Some people there wanted to see Jesus do something wrong so they could accuse him. They watched him closely to see if he would heal the man on the Sabbath[d] day.

[3] Jesus said to the man with the crippled hand, "Stand up here in front of everyone."

[4] Then Jesus asked the people, "Which is right on the Sabbath day: to do good, or to do evil? Is it right to save a life or to destroy one?" But they said nothing to answer him.

[5] Jesus was angry as he looked at the people. But he felt very sad because they were stubborn. Then he said to the man, "Let me see your hand." The man put his hand out for Jesus, and it was healed. [6] Then the Pharisees[d] left and began making plans with the Herodians[n] about a way to kill Jesus.

Many People Follow Jesus

[7] Jesus left with his followers for the lake. A large crowd from Galilee followed him. [8] Also many people came from Judea, from Jerusalem, from Idumea, from the lands across the Jordan River, and from the area of

---

John   John the Baptist who preached to the Jews about Christ's coming (Mark 1:4–8).
giving up eating   This is called "fasting". The people would give up eating for a special time of prayer and worship to God. It was also done to show sadness.
Herodians   A political group that followed Herod and his family.

Tyre and Sidon. They came because they had heard about all the things Jesus was doing. [9] Jesus saw the crowds. So he told his followers to get a boat ready for him. He wanted the boat so that the many people would not crowd themselves against him. [10] He had healed many people. So all the sick were pushing toward him to touch him. [11] Some had evil spirits in them. When the evil spirits saw Jesus, they fell down before him and shouted, "You are the Son of God!" [12] But Jesus strongly commanded the spirits not to tell who he was.

Jesus Chooses His 12 Apostles

[13] Then Jesus went up on a hill and called some men to come to him. These were the men Jesus wanted, and they went up to him. [14] Jesus chose 12 men and called them apostles.[d] He wanted these 12 to be with him, and he wanted to send them to other places to preach. [15] He also wanted them to have the power to force demons[d] out of people. [16] These are the 12 men he chose: Simon (Jesus gave him the name Peter); [17] James and John, the sons of Zebedee (Jesus gave them the name Boanerges, which means "Sons of Thunder"); [18] Andrew, Philip, Bartholomew, Matthew, Thomas, James the son of Alphaeus, Thaddaeus, Simon the Zealot,[d] [19] and Judas Iscariot. Judas is the one who gave Jesus to his enemies.

People Say Jesus Has a Devil

[20] Then Jesus went back home. But again a crowd gathered. There were so many people that Jesus and his followers could not eat. [21] His family heard about all these things. They went to get him because people were saying that Jesus was out of his mind. [22] And the teachers of the law from Jerusalem were saying, "Beelzebul[d] is living inside him! He uses power from the ruler of demons[d] to force demons out."

[23] So Jesus called the people together and used stories to teach them. He said, "Satan will not force his own demons out of people. [24] A kingdom that fights against itself cannot continue, [25] and a family that is divided cannot continue. [26] And if Satan is against himself and fights against his own people, then he cannot continue. And that is the end of Satan. [27] If a person wants to enter a strong man's house and steal his things, first he must tie up the strong man. Then the thief can steal the things from the strong man's house. [28] I tell you the truth. All sins that people do can be forgiven. And all the bad things people say against God can be forgiven. [29] But any person who says bad things against the Holy Spirit[d] will never be forgiven. He is guilty of a sin that continues for ever."

[30] Jesus said this because the teachers of the law said that Jesus had an evil spirit inside him.

Jesus' True Family

[31] Then Jesus' mother and brothers arrived. They stood outside and sent someone in to tell him to come out. [32] Many people were sitting around Jesus. They said to him, "Your mother and brothers are waiting for you outside."

[33] Jesus asked, "Who is my mother? Who are my brothers?" [34] Then Jesus looked at those sitting around him. He said, "Here are my mother and my brothers! [35] My true brother and sister and mother are those who do the things God wants."

A Story About Planting Seed

4 Another time Jesus began teaching by the lake. A great crowd

gathered around him. So he got into a boat and went out on the lake. All the people stayed on the shore close to the water. [2] Jesus used many stories to teach them. He said, [3] "Listen! A farmer went out to plant his seed. [4] While the farmer was planting, some seed fell by the road. The birds came and ate all that seed. [5] Some seed fell on rocky ground where there wasn't much soil. The seed grew very fast there because the ground was not deep. [6] But when the sun rose, the plants withered. The plants died because they did not have deep roots. [7] Some other seed fell among thorny weeds. The weeds grew and choked the good plants. So those plants did not make grain. [8] Some other seed fell on good ground. In the good ground, the seed began to grow. It grew and made a crop of grain. Some plants made 30 times more grain, some 60 times more grain, and some 100 times more grain."

[9] Then Jesus said, "You people who hear me, listen!"

Jesus Tells Why He Used Stories

[10] Later, when Jesus was alone, the 12 apostles[d] and others around him asked him about the stories.

[11] Jesus said, "Only you can know the secret truth about the kingdom of God. But to other people I tell everything by using stories. [12] I do this so that:

'They will look and look, but they
   will not learn.
They will listen and listen, but
   they will not understand.
If they did learn and understand,
   they would come back to me
   and be forgiven'."

Isaiah 6:9–10

Jesus Explains the Seed Story

[13] Then Jesus said to the followers, "Do you understand this story? If you don't, then how will you understand any story? [14] The farmer is like a person who plants God's teaching in people. [15] Sometimes the teaching falls on the road. This is like some people. They hear the teaching of God. But Satan quickly comes and takes away the teaching that was planted in them. [16] Others are like the seed planted on rocky ground. They hear the teaching and quickly accept it with joy. [17] But they don't allow the teaching to go deep into their lives. They keep it only a short time. When trouble or persecution comes because of the teaching, they quickly give up. [18] Others are like the seed planted among thorny weeds. They hear the teaching. [19] But then other things come into their lives: worries, the love of money, and wanting all kinds of other things. These things stop the teaching from growing. So that teaching does not produce fruit[n] in their lives. [20] Others are like the seed planted in the good ground. They hear the teaching and accept it. Then they grow and produce fruit – sometimes 30 times more, sometimes 60 times more, and sometimes 100 times more."

Use What You Have

[21] Then Jesus said to them, "Do you hide a lamp under a bowl or under a bed? No! You put the lamp on a lampstand. [22] Everything that is hidden will be made clear. Every secret thing will be made known. [23] You people who hear me, listen!

[24] "Think carefully about the things you hear. The way you give to others is the way God will give to you. But

---

produce fruit   To produce fruit means to have in your life the good things God wants.

God will give you more than you give. 25The person who has something will be given more. But the person who does not have much, even what he has will be taken from him."

Jesus Uses a Story About Seed

26Then Jesus said, "The kingdom of God is like a man who plants seed in the ground. 27The seed comes up and grows night and day. It doesn't matter whether the man is asleep or awake; the seed still grows. The man does not know how it grows. 28Without any help, the earth produces grain. First the plant grows, then the head, and then all the grain in the head. 29When the grain is ready, the man cuts it. This is the harvest time."

A Story About Mustard Seed

30Then Jesus said, "How can I show you what the kingdom of God is like? What story can I use to explain it? 31The kingdom of God is like a mustard seed. The mustard seed is the smallest seed you plant in the ground. 32But when you plant this seed, it grows and becomes the largest of all garden plants. It produces large branches. Even the wild birds can make nests in it and be protected from the sun."

33Jesus used many stories like these to teach them. He taught them all that they could understand. 34He always used stories to teach them. But when he and his followers were alone together, Jesus explained everything to them.

Jesus Stops a Storm

35That evening, Jesus said to his followers, "Come with me across the lake." 36He and the followers left the people there. They went in the boat that Jesus was already sitting in. There were also other boats with them. 37A very strong wind came up on the lake.

The waves began coming over the sides and into the boat. It was almost full of water. 38Jesus was at the back of the boat, sleeping with his head on a pillow. The followers went to him and woke him. They said, "Teacher, do you care about us? We will drown!"

39Jesus stood up and commanded the wind and the waves to stop. He said, "Quiet! Be still!" Then the wind stopped, and the lake became calm.

40Jesus said to his followers, "Why are you afraid? Do you still have no faith?"

41The followers were very afraid and asked each other, "What kind of man is this? Even the wind and the waves obey him!"

A Man with Demons Inside Him

5 Jesus and his followers went across the lake to the region of the Gerasene people. 2When Jesus got out of the boat, a man came to him from the caves where dead people were buried. This man, who lived in the caves, had an evil spirit living in him. 3No one could tie him up, not even with a chain. 4Many times people had used chains to tie the man's hands and feet. But he always broke the chains off. No one was strong enough to control him. 5Day and night he would wander around the burial caves and on the hills, screaming and cutting himself with stones. 6While Jesus was still far away, the man saw him. He ran to Jesus and knelt down before him. 7-8Jesus said to the man, "You evil spirit, come out of that man."

But the man shouted in a loud voice, "What do you want with me, Jesus, Son of the Most High God? I beg you, promise God that you will not punish me!"

9Then Jesus asked the man, "What is your name?"

The man answered, "My name is

Legion,ⁿ because I have many spirits in me." ¹⁰The man begged Jesus again and again not to send the spirits out of that area.

¹¹A large herd of pigs was eating on a hill near there. ¹²The evil spirits begged Jesus, "Send us to the pigs. Let us go into them." ¹³So Jesus allowed them to do this. The evil spirits left the man and went into the pigs. Then the herd of pigs rushed down the hill into the lake and were drowned. There were about 2,000 pigs in that herd.

Mark 5:13 Then the herd of pigs rushed down the hill into the lake and were drowned.

¹⁴The men who took care of the pigs ran away. They went to the town and to the countryside, telling everyone about this. So people went out to see what had happened. ¹⁵They came to Jesus and saw the man who had had the many evil spirits. The man was sitting there, clothed and in his right mind. The people were frightened. ¹⁶Some people were there who saw what Jesus had done. They told the others what had happened to the man who had the demons^d living in him. And they also told about the pigs. ¹⁷Then the people began to beg Jesus to leave their area.

¹⁸Jesus was getting ready to leave in the boat. The man who was freed from the demons begged to go with him.

¹⁹But Jesus would not allow the man to go. Jesus said, "Go home to your family and friends. Tell them how much the Lord has done for you and how he has had mercy on you." ²⁰So the man left and told the people in the Ten Townsⁿ about the great things Jesus had done for him. All the people were amazed.

Jesus Gives Life to a Dead Girl and Heals a Sick Woman

²¹Jesus went in the boat back to the other side of the lake. There, a large crowd gathered around him. ²²A ruler from the synagogue,^d named Jairus, came to that place. Jairus saw Jesus and bowed before him. ²³The ruler begged Jesus again and again. He said, "My little daughter is dying. Please come and put your hands on her. Then she will be healed and will live." ²⁴So Jesus went with the ruler, and many people followed Jesus. They were pushing very close around him.

²⁵A woman was there who had been bleeding for the past 12 years. ²⁶She had suffered very much. Many doctors had tried to help her. She had spent all the money she had, but she

Legion   Means very many. A legion was about 5,000 men in the Roman army.
Ten Towns   In Greek, called "Decapolis". It was an area east of Lake Galilee that once had ten main towns.

was not improving. She was getting worse. ²⁷When the woman heard about Jesus, she followed him with the people and touched his coat. ²⁸The woman thought, "If I can even touch his coat, that will be enough to heal me." ²⁹When she touched his coat, her bleeding stopped. She could feel in her body that she was healed.

³⁰At once Jesus felt power go out from him. So he stopped and turned around. Then he asked, "Who touched my clothes?"

³¹The followers said, "There are so many people pushing against you! And you ask, 'Who touched me?'"

³²But Jesus continued looking around to see who had touched him. ³³The woman knew that she was healed. So she came and bowed at Jesus' feet. Shaking with fear, she told him the whole story. ³⁴Jesus said to the woman, "Dear woman, you are made well because you believed. Go in peace. You will have no more suffering."

³⁵Jesus was still speaking to her when some men came from the house of Jairus, the synagogue ruler. The men said, "Your daughter is dead. There is now no need to bother the teacher."

³⁶But Jesus paid no attention to what the men said. He said to the synagogue ruler, "Don't be afraid; only believe."

³⁷Jesus let only Peter, James, and John the brother of James go with him to Jairus's house. ³⁸They came to the house of the synagogue ruler, and Jesus found many people there crying loudly. There was much confusion. ³⁹Jesus entered the house and said to the people, "Why are you crying and making so much noise? This child is not dead. She is only asleep." ⁴⁰But they only laughed at Jesus. He told all the people to leave. Then he went into the room where the child was. He took the child's father and mother and his three followers into the room with him. ⁴¹Then he took hold of the girl's hand and said to her, "Talitha, koum!" (This means, "Little girl, I tell you to stand up!") ⁴²The girl stood right up and began walking. (She was 12 years old.) The father and mother and the followers were amazed. ⁴³Jesus gave the father and mother strict orders not to tell people about this. Then he told them to give the girl some food.

Jesus Goes to His Home Town

6 Jesus left there and went back to his home town. His followers went with him. ²On the Sabbath*ᵈ* day he taught in the synagogue.*ᵈ* Many people heard him and were amazed. They said, "Where did this man get these teachings? What is this wisdom that has been given to him? And where did he get the power to work miracles?*ᵈ* ³He is only the carpenter. His mother is Mary. He is the brother of James, Joseph, Judas, and Simon. And his sisters are here with us." The people did not accept Jesus.

⁴Jesus said to them, "Other people give honour to a prophet.*ᵈ* But in his own town with his own people and in his own home, a prophet does not receive honour." ⁵Jesus was not able to work many miracles there. The only miracles he did were to heal some sick people by putting his hands on them. ⁶Jesus was amazed that they had no faith.

Then Jesus went to other villages in that area and taught. ⁷He called the 12 followers together and sent them out in groups of two. He gave them authority over evil spirits. ⁸This is what Jesus told them: "Take nothing for your trip except a walking stick. Take no bread, no bag, and no money in your pockets. ⁹Wear sandals, and take only the clothes you are wearing.

[10] When you enter a house, stay there until you leave that place. [11] If any town refuses to accept you or its people refuse to listen to you, then leave that town. Shake its dust off your feet.[n] This will be a warning to them."

[12] The followers went out and preached to the people to change their hearts and lives. [13] The followers forced many demons[d] out and poured olive oil on many sick people and healed them.

How John the Baptist Was Killed

[14] King Herod heard about Jesus, because Jesus was now well-known. Some people said, "He is John the Baptist.[d] He is risen from death. That is the reason he can work these miracles."[d]

[15] Others said, "He is Elijah."[n]

Other people said, "Jesus is a prophet.[d] He is like the prophets who lived long ago."

[16] Herod heard all these things about Jesus. He said, "I killed John by cutting off his head. Now he has been raised from death!"

[17] Herod himself had ordered his soldiers to arrest John, and John was put in prison. Herod did this to please his wife, Herodias. Herodias was the wife of Philip, Herod's brother. But then Herod married her. [18] John told Herod that it was not lawful for him to be married to his brother's wife. [19] So Herodias hated John and wanted to kill him. But she could not because of Herod. [20] Herod was afraid to kill John because he knew John was a good and holy man. So Herod protected John. Also, Herod enjoyed listening to John preach. But John's preaching always bothered him. [21] Then the perfect time came for Herodias to cause John's death. It happened on Herod's birthday. Herod gave a dinner party for the most important government leaders, the commanders of his army, and the most important people in Galilee. [22] The daughter of Herodias came to the party and danced. When she danced, Herod and the people eating with him were very pleased.

So King Herod said to the girl, "I will give you anything you want." [23] He promised her, "Anything you ask for I will give to you. I will even give you half of my kingdom."

[24] The girl went to her mother and asked, "What should I ask the king to give me?"

Her mother answered, "Ask for the head of John the Baptist."[d]

[25] Quickly the girl went back to the king. She said to him, "Please give me the head of John the Baptist. Bring it to me now on a platter."

[26] The king was very sad. But he had promised to give the girl anything she wanted. And the people eating there with him had heard his promise. So Herod could not refuse what she asked. [27] Immediately the king sent a soldier to bring John's head. The soldier went and cut off John's head in the prison [28] and brought it back on a platter. He gave it to the girl, and the girl gave it to her mother. [29] John's followers heard about what happened. So they came and got John's body and put it in a tomb.

More than 5,000 People Fed

[30] The apostles[d] that Jesus had sent out to preach returned. They gathered around him and told him about all the things they had done and taught. [31] Crowds of people were coming and

---

Shake . . . feet A warning. It showed that they had finished talking to these people.
Elijah A man who spoke for God. He lived hundreds of years before Christ.

going. Jesus and his followers did not even have time to eat. He said to them, "Come with me. We will go to a quiet place to be alone. There we will get some rest."

³²So they went in a boat alone to a place where there were no people. ³³But many people saw them leave and recognised them. So people from all the towns ran to the place where Jesus was going. They got there before Jesus arrived. ³⁴When he landed, he saw a great crowd waiting. Jesus felt sorry for them, because they were like sheep without a shepherd. So he taught them many things.

³⁵It was now late in the day. Jesus' followers came to him and said, "No one lives in this place. And it is already very late. ³⁶Send the people away. They need to go to the farms and towns around here to buy some food to eat."

³⁷But Jesus answered, "You give them food to eat."

They said to him, "We can't buy enough bread to feed all these people! We would all have to work a month to earn enough money to buy that much bread!"

³⁸Jesus asked them, "How many loaves of bread do you have now? Go and see."

When they found out, they came to him and said, "We have five loaves and two fish."

³⁹Then Jesus said to the followers, "Tell all the people to sit in groups on the green grass." ⁴⁰So all the people sat in groups. They sat in groups of 50 or groups of 100. ⁴¹Jesus took the five loaves and two fish. He looked up to heaven and thanked God for the bread. He divided the bread and gave it to his followers for them to give to the people. Then he divided the two fish among them all. ⁴²All the people ate and were satisfied. ⁴³The followers filled 12 baskets with the pieces of bread and fish that were not eaten. ⁴⁴There were about 5,000 men there who ate.

Jesus Walks on the Water

⁴⁵Then Jesus told his followers to get into the boat and go to Bethsaida on the other side of the lake. Jesus said that he would come later. He stayed there to tell the people they could go home. ⁴⁶After sending them away, he went into the hills to pray.

⁴⁷That night, the boat was in the middle of the lake. Jesus was alone on the land. ⁴⁸He saw the followers working hard to row the boat because the wind was blowing against them. At some time between three and six o'clock in the morning, Jesus came to them, walking on the water. He continued walking until he was almost past the boat. ⁴⁹But when his followers saw him walking on the water, they thought he was a ghost and cried out. ⁵⁰They all saw him and were terrified. But Jesus spoke to them and said, "Have courage! It is I! Do not be afraid." ⁵¹Then he got into the boat with them. And the wind became calm. The followers were greatly amazed. ⁵²They had seen Jesus make more bread from the five loaves. But they did not understand what it meant. Their minds were closed.

⁵³When they had crossed the lake, they came to shore at Gennesaret. They tied the boat there. ⁵⁴When they got out of the boat, the people saw Jesus and immediately recognised him. ⁵⁵They ran to tell others everywhere in that area that Jesus was there. They brought sick people on mats to every place Jesus went. ⁵⁶Jesus went into towns and cities and farms around that area. And everywhere he went, the people brought the sick to the marketplaces. They begged him to let them just touch the edge of

his coat. And all who touched him were healed.

Obey God's Law Not Men's

7 Some Pharisees[d] and some teachers of the law came from Jerusalem. They gathered around Jesus. [2]They saw that some of Jesus' followers ate food with hands that were not clean.[d] ("Not clean" means that they did not wash their hands in the way the Pharisees said people must. [3]The Pharisees and all the Jews never eat before washing their hands in this special way. They do this to follow the teaching given to them by their great people who lived before them. [4]And when the Jews buy something in the market, they never eat it until they have washed it in a special way. They also follow other rules of their great people who lived before them. They follow rules about the washing of cups, pitchers, and pots.)

[5]The Pharisees and the teachers of the law said to Jesus, "Your followers don't follow the rules given to us by our great people who lived before us. Your followers eat their food with hands that are not clean. Why do they do this?"

[6]Jesus answered, "You are all hypocrites![d] Isaiah was right when he spoke about you. Isaiah wrote,

'These people show honour to me
     with words.
But their hearts are far from
     me.
[7]Their worship of me is worthless.
The things they teach are
     nothing
but human rules they have
     memorised'.   *Isaiah 29:13*

[8]You have stopped following the commands of God. Now you only follow the teachings of men."

[9]Then Jesus said to them: "You think you are clever! You ignore the commands of God so that you can follow your own teachings! [10]Moses said, 'Honour your father and mother'.[n] Then Moses also said, 'Anyone who says cruel things to his father or mother must be put to death'.[n] [11]But you teach that a person can say to his father or mother, 'I have something I could use to help you. But I will not use it for you. I will give it to God'. [12]You are telling that person that he does not have to do anything for his father or mother. [13]So you are teaching that it is not important to do what God said. You think that it is more important to follow your own rules,

'Honour your father and mother'.   Quotation from Exodus 20:12; Deuteronomy 5:16.
'Anyone . . . death'.   Quotation from Exodus 21:17.

Mark 7:5 "Your followers eat their food with hands that are not clean."

which you teach people. And you do many things like that."

[14] Jesus called the people to him again. He said, "Every person should listen to me and understand what I am saying. [15] There is nothing a person puts into his body that makes him unclean. A person is made unclean by the things that come out of him." [16] [n]

[17] When Jesus left the people and went inside, his followers asked him about this story. [18] Jesus said, "Do you still have trouble understanding? Surely you know that nothing that enters a man from the outside can make him unclean. [19] Food does not go into a person's mind. Food goes into his stomach. Then that food goes out of his body." (When Jesus said this, he meant that there is no food that is unclean for people to eat.)

[20] And Jesus said, "The things that come out of a man are the things that make him unclean. [21] All these evil things begin inside a person, in his mind: evil thoughts, sexual sins, stealing, murder, adultery,[d] [22] selfishness, doing bad things to other people, lying, doing sinful things, jealousy, saying bad things about people, pride, and foolish living. [23] All these evil things come from within a person. These things make a person unclean."

Jesus Helps a Non-Jewish Woman

[24] Jesus left that place and went to the area around Tyre. He went into a house and did not want anyone to know he was there. But Jesus could not stay hidden. [25] A woman heard that he was there. Her little daughter had an evil spirit in her. So the woman quickly came to Jesus and fell at his feet. [26] She was not Jewish. She was Greek, born in Phoenicia, in Syria. She begged Jesus to force the demon[d] out of her daughter.

[27] Jesus told the woman: "It is not right to take the children's bread and give it to the dogs. First let the children eat all they want."

[28] She answered, "That is true, Lord. But the dogs under the table can eat the pieces of food that the children don't eat."

[29] Then Jesus said, "That is a very good answer. You may go. The demon has left your daughter."

[30] The woman went home and found her daughter lying in bed. The demon was gone.

Jesus Heals a Deaf Man

[31] Then Jesus left the area around Tyre. He went through Sidon to Lake Galilee, to the area of the Ten Towns.[n] [32] While he was there, some people brought a man to him. This man was deaf and could not talk. The people begged Jesus to put his hand on the man to heal him.

[33] Jesus led the man away from the crowd, to be alone with him. Jesus put his fingers in the man's ears. Then Jesus spat and touched the man's tongue. [34] Jesus looked up to heaven and took a deep breath. He said to the man, "Ephphatha!" (This means, "Be opened".) [35] When Jesus did this, the man was able to hear. He was also able to use his tongue, and he spoke clearly.

[36] Jesus commanded the people not to tell anyone about what happened. But the more he commanded them, the more they told about it. [37] They were really amazed. They said, "Jesus does everything well. He makes the

---

Verse 16   Some Greek copies add verse 16: "You people who hear me, listen!"
Ten Towns   In Greek, called "Decapolis". It was an area east of Lake Galilee that once had ten main towns.

deaf hear! And those who can't talk – Jesus makes them able to speak."

More than 4,000 People Fed

8 Another time there was a great crowd with Jesus. They had nothing to eat. So Jesus called his followers to him. He said, [2]"I feel sorry for these people. They have been with me for three days, and now they have nothing to eat. [3]I cannot send them home hungry. If they leave without eating, they will faint on the way home. Some of them live a long way from here."

[4]Jesus' followers answered, "But we are far away from any towns. Where can we get enough bread to feed all these people?"

[5]Jesus asked, "How many loaves of bread do you have?"

They answered, "We have seven loaves."

[6]Jesus told the people to sit on the ground. Then he took the seven loaves and gave thanks to God. Jesus divided the bread and gave the pieces to his followers. He told them to pass out the bread to the people, and they did so. [7]The followers also had a few small fish. Jesus gave thanks for the fish and told his followers to give the fish to the people. [8]All the people ate and were satisfied. Then the followers filled seven baskets with the pieces of food that were not eaten. [9]There were about 4,000 men who ate. After they had eaten, Jesus told them to go home. [10]Then he went in a boat with his followers to the area of Dalmanutha.

The Leaders Ask for a Miracle

[11]The Pharisees[d] came to Jesus and asked him questions. They wanted to trap him. So they asked Jesus to do a miracle[d] to show that he was from God. [12]Jesus sighed deeply. He said, "Why do you people ask for a miracle as proof? I tell you the truth. No miracle will be given to you." [13]Then Jesus left the Pharisees. He went in the boat to the other side of the lake.

Guard Against Wrong Teachings

[14]The followers had only one loaf of bread with them in the boat. They had forgotten to bring more bread. [15]Jesus warned them, "Be careful! Guard against the yeast of the Pharisees[d] and the yeast of Herod."

[16]Among themselves, his disciples discussed the meaning of this. They said, "He said this because we have no bread."

[17]Jesus knew what his followers were talking about. So he asked them, "Why are you talking about having no bread? You still don't see or understand? Are your minds closed? [18]You have eyes, but you don't really see. You have ears, but you don't really listen. Remember what I did before, when we did not have enough bread? [19]I divided five loaves of bread for 5,000 people. Remember how many baskets you filled with pieces of food that were not eaten?"

They answered, "We filled 12 baskets."

[20]"And remember that I divided seven loaves of bread for 4,000 people. Remember how many baskets you filled with pieces of food that were not eaten?"

They answered, "We filled seven baskets."

[21]Then Jesus said to them, "You remember these things I did, but you still don't understand?"

Jesus Heals a Blind Man

[22]Jesus and his followers came to Bethsaida. Some people brought a blind man to Jesus and begged him to touch the man. [23]So Jesus took the blind man's hand and led him out of the village. Then he spat on the man's

eyes. He put his hands on the blind man and asked, "Can you see now?" [24]The man looked up and said, "Yes, I see people, but they look like trees walking around."

[25]Again Jesus put his hands on the man's eyes. Then the man opened his eyes wide. His eyes were healed, and he was able to see everything clearly. [26]Jesus told him to go home, saying, "Don't go into the town."

Peter Says Jesus Is the Christ

[27]Jesus and his followers went to the towns around Caesarea Philippi. While they were travelling, Jesus asked them, "Who do people say I am?"

[28]They answered, "Some people say you are John the Baptist.[d] Others say you are Elijah.[n] And others say that you are one of the prophets."[d]

[29]Then Jesus asked, "Who do you say I am?"

Peter answered, "You are the Christ."[d]

[30]Jesus ordered his followers, "Don't tell anyone who I am."

[31]Then Jesus began to teach them that the Son of Man[d] must suffer many things. He taught that the Son of Man would not be accepted by the older Jewish leaders, the leading priests, and the teachers of the law. He taught that the Son of Man must be killed and then rise from death after three days. [32]Jesus told them plainly what would happen. Then Peter took Jesus aside and began to criticise him. [33]But Jesus turned and looked at his followers. Then he criticised Peter and said, "Go away from me, Satan![n] You don't care about the things of God. You care only about things men think are important."

[34]Then Jesus called the crowd to him, along with his followers. He said, "If anyone wants to follow me, he must say 'no' to the things he wants. He must be willing to die on a cross, and he must follow me. [35]Whoever wants to save his life will give up true life. But whoever gives up his life for me and for the Good News[d] will have true life for ever. [36]It is worth nothing for a person to have the whole world, if he loses his soul. [37]A person could never pay enough to buy back his soul. [38]The people who live now are living in a sinful and evil time. If anyone is ashamed of me and my teaching, then I will be ashamed of him. I will be ashamed of him when I come with the glory of my Father and the holy angels."

9 Then Jesus said to the people, "I tell you the truth. Some of you standing here will see the kingdom of God come with power before you die."

Jesus with Moses and Elijah

[2]Six days later Jesus took Peter, James, and John and went up on a high mountain. They were all alone there. While these followers watched, Jesus was changed. [3]His clothes became shining white, whiter than any person could make them. [4]Then two men appeared, talking with Jesus. The men were Moses and Elijah.[n]

[5]Peter said to Jesus, "Teacher, it is good that we are here. We will put three tents here – one for you, one for Moses, and one for Elijah." [6]Peter did not know what to say, because he and the others were so frightened.

[7]Then a cloud came and covered them. A voice came from the cloud.

Elijah   A man who spoke for God. He lived hundreds of years before Christ.
Satan   Name for the devil meaning "the enemy". Jesus means that Peter was talking like Satan.
Moses and Elijah   Two of the most important Jewish leaders in the past.

The voice said, "This is my Son, and I love him. Obey him!"

[8] Then Peter, James, and John looked around, but they saw only Jesus there alone with them.

[9] As Jesus and his followers were walking back down the mountain, he commanded them, "Don't tell anyone about the things you saw on the mountain. Wait till the Son of Man[d] rises from death. Then you may tell."

[10] So the followers obeyed Jesus and said nothing about what they had seen. But they discussed what Jesus meant about rising from death.

[11] They asked Jesus, "Why do the teachers of the law say that Elijah must come first?"

[12] Jesus answered, "They are right to say that Elijah must come first. Elijah makes all things the way they should be. But why does the Scripture[d] say that the Son of Man will suffer much and that people will treat him as if he were nothing? [13] I tell you that Elijah has already come. And people did to him whatever they wanted to do. The Scriptures said this would happen to him."

Jesus Heals a Sick Boy

[14] Then Jesus, Peter, James, and John went to the other followers. They saw a great crowd around them. The teachers of the law were arguing with them. [15] But when the crowd saw Jesus, they were surprised and ran to welcome him.

[16] Jesus asked, "What are you arguing about with the teachers of the law?"

[17] A man answered, "Teacher, I brought my son to you. He has a spirit from the devil in him. This spirit stops him from talking. [18] The spirit attacks him and throws him on the ground. My son foams at the mouth, grinds his teeth, and becomes very stiff. I asked your followers to force the evil spirit out, but they couldn't."

[19] Jesus answered, "You people don't believe! How long must I stay with you? How long must I go on being patient with you? Bring the boy to me!"

[20] So the followers brought him to Jesus. As soon as the evil spirit saw Jesus, it attacked the boy. He fell down and rolled on the ground, foaming from his mouth.

[21] Jesus asked the boy's father, "How long has this been happening?"

The father answered, "Since he was very young. [22] The spirit often throws him into a fire or into water to kill him. If you can do anything for him, please have pity on us and help us."

[23] Jesus said to the father, "You said, 'If you can!' All things are possible for him who believes."

[24] Immediately the father cried out, "I do believe! Help me to believe more!"

[25] Jesus saw that a crowd was running there to see what was happening. So he spoke to the evil spirit, saying, "You deaf and dumb spirit – I command you to come out of this boy and never enter him again!"

[26] The evil spirit screamed and caused the boy to fall on the ground again. Then the spirit came out. The boy looked as if he were dead. And many people said, "He is dead!" [27] But Jesus took hold of the boy's hand and helped him to stand up.

[28] Jesus went into the house. His followers were alone with him there. They said, "Why couldn't we force that evil spirit out?"

[29] Jesus answered, "That kind of spirit can only be forced out by prayer."

Jesus Talks About His Death

[30] Then Jesus and his followers left that place and went through Galilee.

Jesus did not want anyone to know where he was [31]because he wanted to teach his followers alone. He said to them, "The Son of Man[d] will be given to men who will kill him. After three days, he will rise from death." [32]But the followers did not understand what Jesus meant. And they were afraid to ask.

Who Is the Greatest?

[33]Jesus and his followers went to Capernaum and went into a house there. Then Jesus said to them, "What were you arguing about on the road?" [34]But the followers did not answer, because their argument on the road was about which one of them was the greatest.

[35]Jesus sat down and called the 12 apostles[d] to him. He said, "If anyone wants to be the most important, then he must be last of all and servant of all."

[36]Then Jesus took a small child and had him stand among them. He took the child in his arms and said, [37]"If anyone accepts children like these in my name, then he is also accepting me. And if he accepts me, then he is also accepting the One who sent me."

Anyone Not Against Us Is For Us

[38]Then John said, "Teacher, we saw a man using your name to force demons[d] out of a person. We told him to stop, because he does not belong to our group."

[39]Jesus said, "Don't stop him. Anyone who uses my name to do powerful things will not say evil things about me. [40]He who is not against us is with us. [41]I tell you the truth. If anyone

Mark 9:37 "If anyone accepts children . . . he is also accepting me."

helps you by giving you a drink of water because you belong to the Christ,[d] then he will truly get his reward.

[42]"If one of these little children believes in me, and someone causes that child to sin, then it will be very bad for him. It would be better for him to have a large stone tied around his neck and be drowned in the sea. [43]If your hand causes you to sin, cut it off. It is better for you to lose part of your body but have life for ever. That is much better than to have two hands and go to hell. In that place the fire never goes out. [44] [n] [45]If your foot causes you to sin, cut it off. It is better for you to lose part of your body but have life for ever. That is much better than to have two feet and be thrown into hell. [46] [n] [47]If your eye causes you to sin, take it out. It is better for you

Verse 44   Some Greek copies of Mark add verse 44, which is the same as verse 48.
Verse 46   Some Greek copies of Mark add verse 46, which is the same as verse 48.

to have only one eye but have life for ever. That is much better than to have two eyes and be thrown into hell. [48]In hell the worm does not die; the fire is never stopped. [49]Every person will be salted with fire.

[50]"Salt is good. But if the salt loses its salty taste, then you cannot make it salty again. So, be full of goodness. And have peace with each other."

Jesus Teaches About Divorce

10 Then Jesus left that place. He went into the area of Judea and across the Jordan River. Again, crowds came to him. And Jesus taught them as he always did.

[2]Some Pharisees[d] came to Jesus and tried to trick him. They asked, "Is it right for a man to divorce his wife?"

[3]Jesus answered, "What did Moses command you to do?"

[4]They said, "Moses allowed a man to write out divorce papers and send her away."[n]

[5]Jesus said, "Moses wrote that command for you because you refused to accept God's teaching. [6]But when God made the world, 'he made them male and female'.[n] [7]'So a man will leave his father and mother and be united with his wife. [8]And the two people will become one body'.[n] So the people are not two, but one. [9]God has joined the two people together. So no one should separate them."

[10]Later, the followers and Jesus were in the house. They asked Jesus again about the question of divorce. [11]He answered, "Anyone who divorces his wife and marries another woman is guilty of adultery[d] against her. [12]And the woman who divorces her husband and marries another man is also guilty of adultery."

Jesus Accepts Children

[13]Some people brought their small children to Jesus so he could touch them. But his followers told the people to stop bringing their children to him. [14]When Jesus saw this, he was displeased. He said to them, "Let the little children come to me. Don't stop them. The kingdom of God belongs to people who are like these little children. [15]I tell you the truth. You must accept the kingdom of God as a little child accepts things, or you will never enter it." [16]Then Jesus took the children in his arms. He put his hands on them and blessed them.

A Rich Young Man's Question

[17]Jesus started to leave, but a man ran to him and fell on his knees before Jesus. The man asked, "Good teacher, what must I do to get the life that never ends?"

[18]Jesus answered, "Why do you call me good? No one is good except God alone. [19]You know the commands: 'You must not murder anyone. You must not be guilty of adultery.[d] You must not steal. You must not tell lies about your neighbour in court. You must not cheat. Honour your father and mother'."[n]

[20]The man said, "Teacher, I have obeyed all these commands since I was a boy."

[21]Jesus looked straight at the man and loved him. Jesus said, "There is still one more thing you need to do. Go and sell everything you have, and give the money to the poor. You will

---

"Moses . . . away."   Quotation from Deuteronomy 24:1.
'he made . . . female'.   Quotation from Genesis 1:27.
'So . . . body'.   Quotation from Genesis 2:24.
'You . . . mother'.   Quotation from Exodus 20:12–16; Deuteronomy 5:16–20.

have a reward in heaven. Then come and follow me."

²²He was very sad to hear Jesus say this, and he left. The man was sad because he was very rich.

²³Then Jesus looked at his followers and said, "How hard it will be for those who are rich to enter the kingdom of God!"

²⁴The followers were amazed at what Jesus said. But he said again, "My children, it is very hard to enter the kingdom of God! ²⁵And it will be very hard for a rich person to enter the kingdom of God. It would be easier for a camel to go through the eye of a needle!"

²⁶The followers were even more amazed and said to each other, "Then who can be saved?"

²⁷Jesus looked straight at them and said, "This is something that men cannot do. But God can do it. God can do all things."

²⁸Peter said to Jesus, "We left everything to follow you!"

²⁹Jesus said, "I tell you the truth. Everyone who has left his home, brothers, sisters, mother, father, children, or fields for me and for the Good News*d* ³⁰will get a hundred times more than he left. Here in this world he will have more homes, brothers, sisters, mothers, children, and fields. And with those things, he will also suffer for his belief. But in the age that is coming he will have life for ever. ³¹Many who have the highest place now will have the lowest place in the future. And those who have the lowest place now will have the highest place in the future."

Jesus Talks About His Own Death

³²Jesus and the people with him were on the road to Jerusalem. Jesus was leading the way. The followers were amazed, but those who followed behind them were afraid. Jesus took the 12 apostles*d* aside and talked with them alone. He told them what would happen in Jerusalem. ³³He said, "We are going to Jerusalem. The Son of Man*d* will be given to the leading priests and teachers of the law. They will say that he must die. They will give him to the non-Jewish people, ³⁴who will laugh at him and spit on him. They will beat him with whips and kill him. But on the third day after his death, he will rise to life again."

Two Followers Ask Jesus a Favour

³⁵Then James and John, sons of Zebedee, came to Jesus. They said, "Teacher, we want to ask you to do something for us."

³⁶Jesus asked, "What do you want me to do for you?"

³⁷They answered, "You will have glory in your kingdom. Let one of us sit at your right, and let one of us sit at your left."

³⁸Jesus said, "You don't understand what you are asking. Can you drink the cup that I must drink? And can you be baptised with the same kind of baptism that I must have?"*n*

³⁹They answered, "Yes, we can!"

Jesus said to them, "You will drink the same cup that I will drink. And you will be baptised with the same baptism that I must have. ⁴⁰But I cannot choose who will sit at my right or my left. These places are for those for whom they are prepared."

⁴¹The ten followers heard this. They began to be angry with James and John.

⁴²Jesus called all the followers

Can you . . . have? Jesus was asking if they could suffer the same terrible things that would happen to him.

together. He said, "The non-Jewish people have men they call rulers. You know that those rulers love to show their power over the people. And their important leaders love to use all their authority. ⁴³But it should not be that way among you. If one of you wants to become great, then he must serve you like a servant. ⁴⁴If one of you wants to become the most important, then he must serve all of you like a slave. ⁴⁵In the same way, the Son of Man*d* did not come to be served. He came to serve. The Son of Man came to give his life to save many people."

Jesus Heals a Blind Man

⁴⁶Then they came to the town of Jericho. As Jesus was leaving there with his followers and a large crowd, a blind beggar named Bartimaeus (son of Timaeus) was sitting by the road. ⁴⁷He heard that Jesus from Nazareth was walking by. The blind man cried out, "Jesus, Son of David,*d* please help me!"

⁴⁸Many people scolded the blind man and told him to be quiet. But he shouted more and more, "Son of David, please help me!"

⁴⁹Jesus stopped and said, "Tell the man to come here."

So they called the blind man. They said, "Cheer up! Get to your feet. Jesus is calling you." ⁵⁰The blind man stood up quickly. He left his coat there and went to Jesus.

⁵¹Jesus asked him, "What do you want me to do for you?"

The blind man answered, "Teacher, I want to see again."

⁵²Jesus said, "Go. You are healed because you believed." At once the man was able to see again, and he followed Jesus on the road.

Jesus Enters Jerusalem as a King

11 Jesus and his followers were coming closer to Jerusalem. They came to the towns of Bethphage and Bethany near the Mount of Olives.*d* There Jesus sent two of his followers. ²He said to them, "Go to the town you see there. When you enter it, you will find a colt tied which no one has ever ridden. Untie it and bring it here to me. ³If anyone asks you why you are doing this, tell him, 'The Master needs the colt. He will send it back soon'."

⁴The followers went into the town. They found a colt tied in the street near the door of a house, and they untied it. ⁵Some people were standing there and asked, "What are you doing? Why are you untying that colt?" ⁶The followers answered the way Jesus told them to answer, and the people let them take the colt.

⁷The followers brought the colt to Jesus. They put their coats on the colt, and Jesus sat on it. ⁸Many people spread their coats on the road. Others cut branches in the fields and spread the branches on the road. ⁹Some of the people were walking ahead of Jesus. Others were following him. All of them were shouting,

"Praise*n* God!
God bless the One who comes in
    the name of the Lord!

Psalm 118:26

¹⁰God bless the kingdom of our
    father David!
    That kingdom is coming!
Praise to God in heaven!"

¹¹Jesus entered Jerusalem and went into the Temple.*d* When he had looked at everything, and since it was already late, he went out to Bethany with the 12 apostles.*d*

Praise Literally, "Hosanna", a Hebrew word used at first in praying to God for help, but at this time it was probably a shout of joy used in praising God or his Messiah.

[12]The next day as Jesus was leaving Bethany, he was hungry. [13]He saw a fig tree in leaf. So he went to the tree to see if it had any figs on it. But he found no figs, only leaves. It was not the right season for figs to grow. [14]So Jesus said to the tree, "May no one ever eat fruit from you again." Jesus' followers heard him say this.

Jesus Goes to the Temple

[15]Jesus returned to Jerusalem and went into the Temple.[d] He began to throw out those who were buying and selling things there. He overturned the tables that belonged to the men

Mark 11:15 He overturned the tables . . .

who were exchanging different kinds of money. And he turned over the benches of the men who were selling doves. [16]Jesus refused to allow anyone to carry goods through the Temple courts. [17]Then Jesus taught the people. He said, "It is written in the Scriptures,[d] 'My Temple will be a house where people from all nations will pray'.[n] But you are changing God's house into a 'hideout for robbers'."[n]

[18]The leading priests and the teachers of the law heard all this. They began trying to find a way to kill Jesus. They were afraid of him because all the people were amazed at his teaching. [19]That night, Jesus and his followers left the city.

The Power of Faith

[20]The next morning, Jesus was passing by with his followers. They saw the fig tree, and it was dry and dead, even to the roots. [21]Peter remembered the tree and said to Jesus, "Teacher, look! Yesterday, you cursed the fig tree. Now it is dry and dead!"

[22]Jesus answered, "Have faith in God. [23]I tell you the truth. You can say to this mountain, 'Go, mountain, fall into the sea'. And if you have no doubts in your mind and believe that the thing you say will happen, then God will do it for you. [24]So I tell you to ask for things in prayer. And if you believe that you have received those things, then they will be yours. [25]When you are praying, and you remember that you are angry with another person about something, then forgive him. If you do this, then your Father in heaven will also forgive your sins." [26][n]

Leaders Doubt Jesus' Authority

[27]Jesus and his followers went again to Jerusalem. Jesus was walking in the

---

'My Temple . . . pray'. Quotation from Isaiah 56:7.
'hideout for robbers'. Quotation from Jeremiah 7:11.
Verse 26 Some early Greek copies add verse 26: "But if you don't forgive other people, then your Father in heaven will not forgive your sins."

Temple.*d* The leading priests, the teachers of the law, and the older Jewish leaders came to him. ²⁸They said to him, "Tell us! What authority do you have to do these things? Who gave you this authority?" ²⁹Jesus answered, "I will ask you one question. You answer it. Then I will tell you whose authority I use to do these things. ³⁰Tell me: when John baptised people, was that from God or from man? Answer me!" ³¹They argued about Jesus' question. They said to each other, "If we answer, 'John's baptism was from God', then Jesus will say, 'Then why didn't you believe John?' ³²But if we say, 'From man', then the people will be against us." (These leaders were afraid of the people. All the people believed that John was a prophet.*d*) ³³So the leaders answered Jesus, "We don't know."

Jesus said, "Then I will not tell you what authority I use to do these things."

God Sends His Son

12 Jesus used stories to teach the people. He said, "A man planted a vineyard. He put a wall around it and dug a hole for a winepress.*d* Then he built a tower. He leased the vineyard to some farmers and left for a trip. ²Later, it was time for the grapes to be picked. So the man sent a servant to the farmers to get his share of the grapes. ³But the farmers grabbed the servant and beat him. They sent him away with nothing. ⁴Then the man sent another servant. They hit him on the head and showed no respect for him. ⁵So the man sent another servant. They killed this servant. The man sent many other servants. The farmers beat some of them and killed others.

⁶"The man had one person left to send, his son whom he loved. He sent him last of all, saying, 'The farmers will respect my son'.

⁷"But they said to each other, 'This is the owner's son. This vineyard will be his. If we kill him, then it will be ours'. ⁸So they took the son, killed him, and threw him out of the vineyard.

⁹"So what will the man who owns the vineyard do? He will go to the vineyard and kill those farmers. Then he will give the vineyard to other farmers. ¹⁰Surely you have read this Scripture:*d*

'The stone that the builders did
    not want
    became the cornerstone.*d*
¹¹The Lord did this,
    and it is wonderful to us'."
                              Psalm 118:22–23

¹²The Jewish leaders knew that the story was about them. So they wanted to find a way to arrest Jesus, but they were afraid of the people. So the leaders left him and went away.

The Leaders Try to Trap Jesus

¹³Later, the Jewish leaders sent some Pharisees*d* and some men from the group called Herodians*n* to Jesus. They wanted to catch Jesus saying something wrong. ¹⁴They came to him and said, "Teacher, we know that you are an honest man. You are not afraid of what other people think about you. All men are the same to you. And you teach the truth about God's way. Tell us: is it right to pay taxes to Caesar?*d* Should we pay them, or not?"

¹⁵But Jesus knew what these men were really trying to do. He said, "Why are you trying to trap me? Bring me a silver coin. Let me see it." ¹⁶They gave Jesus a coin, and he asked,

Herodians   A political group that followed Herod and his family.

"Whose picture is on the coin? And whose name is written on it?"

They answered, "Caesar's."

[17]Then Jesus said to them, "Give to Caesar the things that are Caesar's. And give to God the things that are God's." The men were amazed at what Jesus said.

Sadducees Try to Trick Jesus

[18]Then some Sadducees[d] came to Jesus. (Sadducees believe that no person will rise from death.) The Sadducees asked Jesus a question. [19]They said, "Teacher, Moses wrote that a man's brother might die. He leaves a wife but no children. Then that man must marry the widow and have children for the dead brother. [20]There were seven brothers. The first brother married but died. He had no children. [21]So the second brother married the widow. But he also died and had no children. The same thing happened with the third brother. [22]All seven brothers married her and died. None of the brothers had any children. The woman was last to die. [23]But all seven brothers had married her. So at the time people rise from death, whose wife will the woman be?"

[24]Jesus answered, "Why did you make this mistake? Is it because you don't know what the Scriptures[d] say? Or is it because you don't know about the power of God? [25]When people rise from death, there will be no marriage. People will not be married to each other but will be like angels in heaven. [26]Surely you have read what God said about people rising from death. In the book in which Moses wrote about the burning bush,[n] it says that God told Moses this: 'I am the God of Abraham, the God of Isaac, and the God of Jacob'.[n] [27]God is the God of living people, not dead people. You Sadducees are wrong!"

The Most Important Command

[28]One of the teachers of the law came to Jesus. He heard Jesus arguing with the Sadducees[d] and the Pharisees.[d] He saw that Jesus gave good answers to their questions. So he asked Jesus, "Which of the commands is most important?"

[29]Jesus answered, "The most important command is this: 'Listen, people of Israel! The Lord our God, he is the only Lord. [30]Love the Lord your God. Love him with all your heart, all your soul, all your mind, and all your strength'.[n] [31]The second most important command is this: 'Love your neighbour as you love yourself'.[n] These two commands are the most important commands."

[32]The man answered, "That was a good answer, Teacher. You were right when you said these things. God is the only Lord, and there is no other God besides him. [33]A person must love God with all his heart, all his mind, and all his strength. And he must love his neighbour as he loves himself. These commands are more important than all the animals and sacrifices we offer to God."

[34]Jesus saw that the man answered him wisely. So Jesus said to him, "You are close to the kingdom of God." And after that, no one was brave enough to ask Jesus any more questions.

[35]Jesus was teaching in the Temple.[d] He asked, "Why do the

---

burning bush   Read Exodus 3:1–12 in the Old Testament.
'I am . . . Jacob'.   Quotation from Exodus 3:6.
'Listen . . . strength'.   Quotation from Deuteronomy 6:4–5.
'Love . . . yourself'.   Quotation from Leviticus 19:18.

teachers of the law say that the Christ[d] is the son of David? [36]David himself, speaking by the Holy Spirit,[d] said:

'The Lord said to my Lord:
Sit by me at my right side,
until I put your enemies under
    your control'.   *Psalm 110:1*

[37]David himself calls the Christ 'Lord'. So how can the Christ be David's son?" The large crowd listened to Jesus with pleasure.

[38]Jesus continued teaching. He said, "Beware of the teachers of the law. They like to walk around wearing clothes that look important. And they love people to show respect to them in the marketplaces. [39]They love to have the most important seats in the synagogues.[d] And they love to have the most important seats at the feasts. [40]They cheat widows and steal their homes. Then they try to make themselves look good by saying long prayers. God will punish these people terribly."

True Giving

[41]Jesus sat near the Temple[d] money box where people put their gifts. He watched the people put in their money. Many rich people gave large sums of money. [42]Then a poor widow came and gave two very small copper coins. These coins were not worth even a penny. [43]Jesus called his followers to him. He said, "I tell you the truth. This poor widow gave only two small coins. But she really gave more than all those rich people. [44]The rich have plenty; they gave only what they did not need. This woman is very poor, but she gave all she had. And she needed that money to help her live."

The Temple Will Be Destroyed

13 Jesus was leaving the Temple.[d] One of his followers said to him,

"Look, Teacher! This Temple has beautiful buildings with very big stones."

[2]Jesus said, "Do you see all these great buildings? Every stone will be thrown to the ground. Not one stone will be left on another."

[3]Later, Jesus was sitting on the Mount of Olives.[d] He was alone with Peter, James, John, and Andrew. They could all see the Temple. They asked Jesus, [4]"Tell us, when will all these things happen? And what will show us that the time has come for them to happen?"

[5]Jesus said to them: "Be careful that no one fools you. [6]Many people will come and use my name. They will say, 'I am the One'. And they will fool many. [7]You will hear about wars and stories of wars that are coming. But don't be afraid. These things must happen before the end comes. [8]Nations will fight against other nations. Kingdoms will fight against other kingdoms. There will be times when there is no food for people to eat. And there will be earthquakes in different places. These things are like the first pains when something new is about to be born.

[9]"You must be careful. People will arrest you and take you to court. They will beat you in their synagogues.[d] You will be forced to stand before kings and governors, to tell them about me. This will happen to you because you follow me. [10]But before these things happen, the Good News[d] must be told to all people. [11]When you are arrested and judged, don't worry about what you should say. Say the things God gives you to say at that time. It will not really be you speaking. It will be the Holy Spirit.[d]

[12]"Brothers will turn against their own brothers and give them over to be killed. Fathers will turn against

their own children and give them over to be killed. Children will fight against their own parents and cause their parents to be killed. [13] All people will hate you because you follow me. But the person who continues to be strong until the end will be saved.

[14] "You will see 'the horrible thing that destroys'.[n] You will see this thing standing in the place where it should not be." (You who read this should understand what it means.) "At that time, the people in Judea should run away to the mountains. [15] If a person is on the roof[n] of his house, he must not go down to take anything out of his house. [16] If a person is in the field, he must not go back to get his coat. [17] At that time, it will be hard for women who are pregnant or have nursing babies. [18] Pray that these things will not happen in winter. [19] This is because those days will be full of trouble. There will be more trouble than there has ever been since the beginning, when God made the world. And nothing as bad will ever happen again. [20] God has decided to make that terrible time short. If that time were not made short, then no one would go on living. But God will make that time short to help his special people whom he has chosen. [21] At that time, someone might say to you, 'Look, there is the Christ!'[d] Or another person might say, 'There he is!' But don't believe them. [22] False Christs and false prophets[d] will come and perform great wonders and miracles.[d] They will do these things to the people God has chosen. They will do these things to try to fool them, if that is possible. [23] So be careful. For I have warned you about all this before it happens.

[24] "During the days after this trouble comes,

'The sun will grow dark.
And the moon will not give its
    light.
[25] The stars will fall from the sky.
And everything in the sky will
    be changed'.   Isaiah 13:10; 34:4

[26] "Then people will see the Son of Man[d] coming in clouds with great power and glory. [27] The Son of Man will send his angels all around the earth. They will gather his chosen people from every part of the earth.

[28] "The fig tree teaches us a lesson: when its branches become green and soft, and new leaves begin to grow, then you know that summer is near. [29] So also when you see all these things happening, then you will know that the time is near, ready to come. [30] I tell you the truth. All these things will happen while the people of this time are still living. [31] The whole world, earth and sky, will be destroyed, but the words I have said will never be destroyed.

[32] "No one knows when that day or time will be. The Son and the angels in heaven don't know. Only the Father knows. [33] Be careful! Always be ready! You don't know when that time will be. [34] It is like a man who goes on a trip. He leaves his house and lets his servants take care of it. He gives each servant a special job to do. One servant has the work of guarding the door. The man tells this servant always to be watchful. This is what I am now telling you. [35] You must always be ready. You don't know when the

---

'horrible . . . destroys.'   Mentioned in Daniel 9:27; 12:11 (cf. Daniel 11:31).
roof   In Bible times houses were built with flat roofs. The roof was used for drying things such as flax and fruit. It was also used as an extra room, as a place for worship and as a place to sleep in the summer.

owner of the house will come back. He might come in the evening, or at midnight, or in the early morning, or when the sun rises. 36 He might come back quickly. If you are always ready, then he will not find you sleeping. 37 I tell you this, and I say this to everyone: 'Be ready!' "

The Plan to Kill Jesus

14 It was now only two days before the Passover[d] and the Feast[d] of Unleavened Bread. The leading priests and teachers of the law were trying to find a way to use some trick to arrest Jesus and kill him. 2 But they said, "We must not do it during the feast. The people might cause a riot."

A Woman with Perfume for Jesus

3 Jesus was in Bethany. He was at dinner in the house of Simon, who had a harmful skin disease. While Jesus was there, a woman came to him. She had an alabaster[d] jar filled with very expensive perfume, made of pure nard.[d] The woman opened the jar and poured the perfume on Jesus' head.

4 Some of those who were there saw this and became angry. They complained to each other, saying, "Why waste that perfume? 5 It was worth a full year's work. It could be sold, and the money could be given to the poor." They spoke to the woman sharply.

6 Jesus said, "Don't bother the woman. Why are you troubling her? She did a beautiful thing for me. 7 You will always have the poor with you. You can help them whenever you want. But you will not always have me. 8 This woman did the only thing she could do for me. She poured perfume on my body. She did this before I die to prepare me for burial. 9 I tell you the truth. The Good News[d] will be told to people in all the world. And in every

Mark 14:3 The woman opened the jar and poured the perfume on Jesus' head.

place it is preached, what this woman has done will be told. And people will remember her."

Judas Becomes an Enemy of Jesus

10 One of the 12 followers, Judas Iscariot, went to talk to the leading priests. Judas offered to give Jesus to them. 11 The leading priests were pleased about this. They promised to pay Judas money. So he waited for the best time to give Jesus to them.

Jesus Eats the Passover Feast

12 It was now the first day of the Feast[d] of Unleavened Bread. This was a time when the Jews always sacrificed the Passover[d] lambs. Jesus' followers came to him. They said, "We will go and prepare everything for the Passover Feast. Where do you want to eat the feast?"

13 Jesus sent two of his followers and said to them, "Go into the city. A man

carrying a jar of water will meet you. Follow him. [14] He will go into a house. Tell the owner of the house, 'The Teacher asks that you show us the room where he and his followers can eat the Passover Feast'. [15] The owner will show you a large room upstairs. This room is ready. Prepare the food for us there."

[16] So the followers left and went into the city. Everything happened as Jesus had said. So they prepared the Passover Feast.

[17] In the evening, Jesus went to that house with the 12. [18] While they were all eating, Jesus said, "I tell you the truth. One of you will give me to my enemies – one of you eating with me now."

[19] The followers were very sad to hear this. Each one said to Jesus, "I am not the one, am I?"

[20] Jesus answered, "The man who is against me is one of the 12. He is the one who dips his bread into the bowl with me. [21] The Son of Man[d] must go and die. The Scriptures[d] say this will happen. But how terrible it will be for the person who gives the Son of Man to be killed. It would be better for that person if he had never been born."

The Lord's Supper

[22] While they were eating, Jesus took some bread. He thanked God for it and broke it. Then he gave it to his followers and said, "Take it. This bread is my body."

[23] Then Jesus took a cup. He thanked God for it and gave it to the followers. All the followers drank from the cup.

[24] Then Jesus said, "This is my blood which begins the new agreement that God makes with his people. This blood is poured out for many. [25] I tell you the truth. I will not drink of this fruit of the vine[n] again until that day when I drink it new in the kingdom of God."

[26] They sang a hymn and went out to the Mount of Olives.[d]

Jesus' Followers Will All Leave Him

[27] Then Jesus told the followers, "You will all lose your faith in me. It is written in the Scriptures:[d]
'I will kill the shepherd,
  and the sheep will scatter'.

Zechariah 13:7

[28] But after I rise from death, I will go ahead of you into Galilee."

[29] Peter said, "All the other followers may lose their faith. But I will not."

[30] Jesus answered, "I tell you the truth. Tonight you will say you don't know me. You will say this three times before the cock crows twice."

[31] But Peter answered strongly, "I will never say that I don't know you! I will even die with you!" And all the other followers said the same thing.

Jesus Prays Alone

[32] Jesus and his followers went to a place called Gethsemane. He said to his followers, "Sit here while I pray." [33] Jesus told Peter, James, and John to come with him. Then Jesus began to be very sad and troubled. [34] He said to them, "I am full of sorrow. My heart is breaking with sadness. Stay here and watch."

[35] Jesus walked a little further away from them. Then he fell on the ground and prayed. He prayed that, if possible, he would not have this time of suffering. [36] He prayed, "Abba,[n] Father! You can do all things. Let me

---

fruit of the vine Product of the grapevine; this may also be translated "wine".
Abba Name that a child called his father.

not have this cup[n] of suffering. But do what you want, not what I want."

[37]Then Jesus went back to his followers. He found them asleep. He said to Peter, "Simon, why are you sleeping? You could not stay awake with me for one hour? [38]Stay awake and pray that you will not be tempted. Your spirit wants to do what is right, but your body is weak."

[39]Again Jesus went away and prayed the same thing. [40]Then he went back to the followers. Again he found them asleep because their eyes were very heavy. And they did not know what to say to Jesus.

[41]After Jesus prayed a third time, he went back to his followers. He said to them, "You are still sleeping and resting? That's enough! The time has come for the Son of Man[d] to be given to sinful people. [42]Get up! We must go. Here comes the man who has turned against me."

Jesus Is Arrested

[43]While Jesus was still speaking, Judas came up. Judas was one of the 12 followers. He had many people with him. They were sent from the leading priests, the teachers of the law, and the older Jewish leaders. Those with Judas had swords and clubs.

[44]Judas had planned a signal for them. He had said, "The man I kiss is Jesus. Arrest him and guard him while you lead him away." [45]So Judas went to Jesus and said, "Teacher!" and kissed him. [46]Then the men grabbed Jesus and arrested him. [47]One of the followers standing near drew his sword. He struck the servant of the high priest with the sword and cut off his ear.

[48]Then Jesus said, "You came to get me with swords and clubs as if I were a criminal. [49]Every day I was with you teaching in the Temple.[d] You did not arrest me there. But all these things have happened to make the Scriptures[d] come true." [50]Then all of Jesus' followers left him and ran away.

[51]A young man, wearing only a linen cloth, was following Jesus. The people also grabbed him. [52]But the cloth he was wearing came off, and he ran away naked.

Jesus Before the Leaders

[53]The people who arrested Jesus led him to the house of the high priest. All the leading priests, the older Jewish leaders, and the teachers of the law were gathered there. [54]Peter followed far behind and entered the courtyard of the high priest's house. There he sat with the guards, warming himself by the fire.

[55]The leading priests and all the Jewish council tried to find something that Jesus had done wrong so they could kill him. But the council could find no proof against him. [56]Many people came and told false things about him. But all said different things – none of them agreed.

[57]Then some men stood up and lied about Jesus. They said, [58]"We heard this man say, 'I will destroy this Temple[d] that men made. And three days later, I will build another Temple – a Temple not made by men'." [59]But even the things these men said did not agree.

[60]Then the high priest stood before them and said to Jesus, "Aren't you going to answer the charges these men bring against you?" [61]But Jesus said nothing. He did not answer.

The high priest asked Jesus another

---

cup   Jesus is talking about the bad things that will happen to him. Accepting these things will be very hard, like drinking a cup of something that tastes very bitter.

question: "Are you the Christ,*d* the Son of the blessed God?"

⁶²Jesus answered, "I am. And in the future you will see the Son of Man*d* sitting at the right side of the Powerful One. And you will see the Son of Man coming on clouds in the sky."

⁶³When the high priest heard this, he was very angry. He tore his clothes and said, "We don't need any more witnesses! ⁶⁴You all heard him say these things against God. What do you think?"

They all said that Jesus was guilty and should be killed. ⁶⁵Some of the people there spat at Jesus. They covered his eyes and hit him with their fists. They said, "Prove that you are a prophet!"*d* Then the guards led Jesus away and beat him.

Peter Says He Doesn't Know Jesus

⁶⁶Peter was still in the courtyard when a servant girl of the high priest came there. ⁶⁷She saw Peter warming himself at the fire. She looked closely at him.

Then the girl said, "You were with Jesus, that man from Nazareth."

⁶⁸But Peter said that he was never with Jesus. He said, "I don't know or understand what you are talking about." Then Peter left and went toward the entrance of the courtyard.*n*

⁶⁹The servant girl saw Peter there. Again she said to the people who were standing there, "This man is one of those who followed Jesus." ⁷⁰Again Peter said that it was not true.

A short time later, some people were standing near Peter. They said, "We know you are one of those who followed Jesus. You are from Galilee, too."

⁷¹Then Peter began to curse. He said, "I swear that I don't know this man you're talking about!"

⁷²As soon as Peter said this, the cock crowed the second time. Then Peter remembered what Jesus had told him: "Before the cock crows twice, you will say three times that you don't know me." Then Peter was very sad and began to cry.

Pilate Questions Jesus

15 Very early in the morning, the leading priests, the older Jewish leaders, the teachers of the law, and all the Jewish council decided what to do with Jesus. They tied him, led him away, and turned him over to Pilate, the governor.

²Pilate asked Jesus, "Are you the king of the Jews?"

Jesus answered, "Yes, I am."

³The leading priests accused Jesus of many things. ⁴So Pilate asked Jesus another question. He said, "You can see that these people are accusing you of many things. Why don't you answer?"

⁵But Jesus still said nothing. Pilate was very surprised at this.

Pilate Tries to Free Jesus

⁶Every year at the Passover*d* time the governor would free one person from prison. He would free any person the people wanted him to free. ⁷At that time, there was a man named Barabbas in prison. He was a rebel and had committed murder during a riot. ⁸The crowd came to Pilate and asked him to free a prisoner as he always did.

⁹Pilate asked them, "Do you want me to free the king of the Jews?" ¹⁰Pilate knew that the leading priests had given Jesus to him because they were jealous of Jesus. ¹¹And the leading

Verse 68   Many Greek copies add: "And the cock crowed."

priests had persuaded the people to ask Pilate to free Barabbas, not Jesus.

¹²Pilate asked the crowd again, "So what should I do with this man you call the king of the Jews?"

¹³They shouted, "Kill him on a cross!"

¹⁴Pilate asked, "Why? What wrong has he done?"

But they shouted louder and louder, "Kill him on a cross!"

¹⁵Pilate wanted to please the crowd. So he freed Barabbas for them. And Pilate told the soldiers to beat Jesus with whips. Then he gave Jesus to the soldiers to be killed on a cross.

¹⁶Pilate's soldiers took Jesus into the governor's palace (called the Praetorium). They called all the other soldiers together. ¹⁷They put a purple robe on Jesus. Then they used thorny branches to make a crown. They put it on his head. ¹⁸Then they called out to him, "Hail, King of the Jews!" ¹⁹The soldiers beat Jesus on the head many times with a stick. They also spat on him. Then they made fun of him by bowing on their knees and worshipping him. ²⁰After they had finished making fun of him, the soldiers took off the purple robe and put his own clothes on him again. Then they led Jesus out of the palace to be killed on a cross.

Jesus Is Killed on a Cross

²¹There was a man from Cyrene coming from the fields to the city. The man was Simon, the father of Alexander and Rufus. The soldiers forced Simon to carry the cross for Jesus. ²²They led Jesus to the place called Golgotha. (Golgotha means the Place of the Skull.) ²³At Golgotha the soldiers tried to give Jesus wine to drink. This wine was mixed with myrrh.^{d} But he refused to drink it. ²⁴The soldiers nailed Jesus to a cross. Then they divided his clothes among themselves. They threw lots^d to decide which clothes each soldier would get.

²⁵It was nine o'clock in the morning when they nailed Jesus to the cross. ²⁶There was a sign with the charge against Jesus written on it. The sign read: "THE KING OF THE JEWS". ²⁷They also put two robbers on crosses beside Jesus, one on the right, and the other on the left. ²⁸ ⁿ ²⁹People walked by and insulted Jesus. They shook their heads, saying, "You said you could destroy the Temple^d and build it again in three days. ³⁰So save yourself! Come down from that cross!"

Verse 28 Some Greek copies add verse 28: "And the Scripture came true that says, 'They put him with criminals'."

Mark 15:20 Then they led Jesus out of the palace to be killed on a cross.

[31] The leading priests and the teachers of the law were also there. They made fun of Jesus just as the other people did. They said among themselves, "He saved other people, but he can't save himself. [32] If he is really the Christ,[d] the king of Israel, then let him come down from the cross now. We will see this, and then we will believe in him." The robbers who were being killed on the crosses beside Jesus also insulted him.

Jesus Dies

[33] At noon the whole country became dark. This darkness lasted for three hours. [34] At three o'clock Jesus cried in a loud voice, "Eloi, Eloi, lama sabachthani." This means, "My God, my God, why have you left me alone?"

[35] Some of the people standing there heard this. They said, "Listen! He is calling Elijah."

[36] One man there ran and got a sponge. He filled the sponge with vinegar and tied it to a stick. Then he used the stick to give the sponge to Jesus to drink from it. The man said, "We should wait now and see if Elijah will come to take him down from the cross."

[37] Then Jesus cried in a loud voice and died.

[38] When Jesus died, the curtain in the Temple[n] split into two pieces. The tear started at the top and tore all the way to the bottom. [39] The army officer that was standing there before the cross saw what happened when Jesus died. The officer said, "This man really was the Son of God!"

[40] Some women were standing at a distance from the cross, watching. Some of these women were Mary Magdalene, Salome, and Mary the mother of James and Joseph. (James was her youngest son.) [41] These were the women who followed Jesus in Galilee and cared for him. Many other women were also there who had come with Jesus to Jerusalem.

Jesus Is Buried

[42] This was Preparation[d] Day. (That means the day before the Sabbath[d] day.) It was becoming dark. [43] A man named Joseph from Arimathea was brave enough to go to Pilate and ask for Jesus' body. Joseph was an important member of the Jewish council. He was one of the people who wanted the kingdom of God to come. [44] Pilate wondered if Jesus was already dead. Pilate called the army officer who guarded Jesus and asked him if Jesus had already died. [45] The officer told Pilate that he was dead. So Pilate told Joseph he could have the body. [46] Joseph bought some linen cloth, took the body down from the cross and wrapped it in the linen. He put the body in a tomb that was cut in a wall of rock. Then he closed the tomb by rolling a very large stone to cover the entrance. [47] And Mary Magdalene and Mary the mother of Joseph saw the place where Jesus was laid.

Jesus Rises from Death

16 The day after the Sabbath[d] day, Mary Magdalene, Mary the mother of James, and Salome bought some sweet-smelling spices to put on Jesus' body. [2] Very early on that day, the first day of the week, the women were on their way to the tomb. It was soon after sunrise. [3] They said to each

---

curtain in the Temple A curtain divided the Most Holy Place from the other part of the Temple. That was the special building in Jerusalem where God commanded the Jews to worship him.

other, "There is a large stone covering the entrance of the tomb. Who will move the stone for us?"

⁴Then the women looked and saw that the stone had already been moved. The stone was very large, but it had been moved away from the entrance. ⁵The women entered the tomb and saw a young man wearing a white robe. He was sitting on the right side, and the women were afraid.

⁶But the man said, "Don't be afraid. You are looking for Jesus from Nazareth, the one who was killed on a cross. He has risen from death. He is not here. Look, here is the place they laid him. ⁷Now go and tell his followers and Peter, 'Jesus is going into Galilee. He will be there before you. You will see him there as he told you before'."

⁸The women were confused and shaking with fear. They left the tomb and ran away. They did not tell anyone about what happened, because they were afraid. ⁿ

Some Followers See Jesus

⁹Jesus rose from death early on the first day of the week. He showed himself first to Mary Magdalene. Once in the past, he had forced seven demons ᵈ to leave Mary. ¹⁰After Mary saw Jesus, she went and told his followers. They were very sad and were crying. ¹¹But Mary told them that Jesus was alive. She said that she had seen him, but the followers did not believe her.

¹²Later, Jesus showed himself to two of his followers while they were walking in the country. But Jesus did not look the same as before. ¹³These followers went back to the others and told them what had happened. Again, the followers did not believe them.

Jesus Talks to the Apostles

¹⁴Later Jesus showed himself to the 11 followers while they were eating. He criticised them because they had little faith. They were stubborn and refused to believe those who had seen him after he had risen from death.

¹⁵Jesus said to the followers, "Go everywhere in the world. Tell the Good News ᵈ to everyone. ¹⁶Anyone who believes and is baptised will be saved. But he who does not believe will be judged guilty. ¹⁷And those who believe will be able to do these things as proof: they will use my name to force demons ᵈ out of people. They will speak in languages ⁿ they never learned. ¹⁸They will pick up snakes without being hurt. And they will drink poison without being hurt. They will touch the sick, and the sick will be healed."

¹⁹After the Lord Jesus said these things to the followers, he was carried up into heaven. There, Jesus sat at the right side of God. ²⁰The followers went everywhere in the world and told the Good News to people. And the Lord helped them. The Lord proved that the Good News they told was true by giving them power to work miracles. ᵈ

Verse 8   Some early Greek copies end the book with verse 8.
languages   This can also be translated "tongues".

DICTIONARY

A

Abba (AB-uh) was a child's word for 'father' in the Aramaic language. Early Christians used this word in speaking to God. This shows how close we can feel to Him. (Mark 14:36; 34:18; Deuteronomy 16:1)

adultery (ah-DUL-ter-ee) is breaking a marriage promise by having sexual relations with someone other than your husband or wife. (Mark 10:11, 12; John 8:3–5)

Andrew (AN-droo) was a fisherman and the brother of the apostle Peter. Andrew was also one of the 12 apostles of Jesus. (Mark 1:16–18; 3:14–19; John 1:40–44; Acts 1:13)

apostle (uh-POS-'l) is a Greek word that means 'someone who is sent off'. Jesus gave the name to the 12 men he chose as his special followers. He sent them to tell the good news about him to the whole world. Later, after Judas killed himself, Matthias became an apostle. Paul was also called an apostle. (Matthew 10:1–4; Mark 3:14–19; Acts 1:2–26; 1 Corinthians 15:8–10)

B

Barabbas (bah-RAB-us) means 'son of a father'. He was a robber who had murdered someone in Jerusalem. He was in jail when Jesus was on trial. It was the time of year when a criminal would be freed from prison. The people cried out to have Barabbas freed and Jesus killed on the cross. Pilate, the Roman governor, did as they demanded. (Matthew 27:16–26; Mark 15:6–11)

Beelzebul (bee-EL-ze-bull), also spelled Beelzebub, came from the name Baal-Zebub. This was the name of the false god of the Philistines. In the New Testament Beelzebul is a name sometimes used for the devil. (Matthew 12:24; Mark 3:22, 23)

C

Christ (KRYST) means 'anointed (or chosen) one' in Greek. In Hebrew the word is 'Messiah'. Jesus is the Christ. He was chosen by God to save people from their sins. (Mark 8:29; 14:61, 62; Luke 23:2; Acts 2:36; 17:3; 18:28)

G

Gethsemane (geth-SEM-uh-nee) was a garden of olive trees just outside Jerusalem. It was at the bottom of the Mount of Olives. The night before Jesus was killed, he prayed in this garden. Jesus was there when Judas brought the soldiers to arrest him. (Matthew 26:36–50; Mark 14:32)

Golgotha (GOL-goh-thuh) is an Aramaic word meaning 'skull'. The Latin word for it is 'Calvary'. This is the hill where Jesus was killed on the cross by the Roman soldiers. It may have been called the 'place of the skull' because many people died there. Or it may have been called that because the hill looked like a giant skull. (Matthew 27:32–35; Mark 15:22–24; John 19:17, 18)

Good News is also called the gospel. In the New Testament, the Good News is that Jesus died for us on the cross, was buried in a tomb, and came back to life. Because he did these things for us, we can be saved. That is good news. (Mark 1:1; Acts 20:24; Colossians 1:21–23; 2 Timothy 1:10)

H

heart in the Bible usually means the mind or feelings. It is not talking about the physical heart that pumps blood through the body. (Mark 12:30; Luke 2:19; 6:45; 12:34; Acts 2:46)

Herod Antipas was the son of Herod I. He had John the Baptist's head cut off. Later, Jesus was sent to this man for trial. He ruled from the year 4 B.C. to about A.D. 39. (Matthew 14:1; Mark 6:14; Luke 23:6–12)

I

Isaac (EYE-zak) means 'laughter'. He was the son of Abraham and Sarah. He was named Isaac because Sarah laughed when the angel told her she would have a baby. She thought she was too old. God tested Abraham by asking him to offer Isaac as a sacrifice on an altar. When God saw that Abraham would obey him, he saved Isaac's life. (Mark 12:26; Hebrews 11:17–20)

J

James, the son of Zebedee was an apostle of Jesus and a brother of the apostle John. He was killed by Herod Agrippa I. (Matthew 10:2; Mark 10:35, 41; Acts 12:2)

John, the apostle was one of the sons of Zebedee. He and his brother James were fishermen. He wrote the gospel of John, the books of 1, 2 and 3 John and probably Revelation. He is sometimes referred to as 'the one Jesus loved'. John, Peter and James were Jesus' closest friends. (Mark 1:19, 20; 9:2; 14:33, 34; Acts 3:1–11; Revelation 1:1–4, 9)

Joseph of Arimathea took the body of Jesus down from the cross and buried it in a tomb he had dug for himself. He was a member of the Jewish religious court called the Sanhedrin. He was probably a Christian. (Matthew 27:57–60; Mark 15:43–46)

M

Mary Magdalene was from the town of Magdala. She was a follower of Jesus. She watched the men put Jesus' body in the tomb. She was the first person to see Jesus after he came back to life. (Matthew 27:56, 61; Mark 15:40, 47; 16:1, 9; John 20:1–18)

myrrh (MUR) was a sweet-smelling liquid taken from certain trees and shrubs. It was used as a perfume and as a pain reliever. It was one of the gifts the wise men gave Jesus when he was born. (Matthew 2:11; Mark 15:23; John 19:39)

N

nard was an expensive perfume. It was expensive because it had to be imported from India. (Mark 14:3; John 12:3)

NARD

P

parable (PAR-uh-b'l) is a story that teaches a lesson by comparing two things. Jesus often used parables to teach the people. Some examples of parables can be found in Mark 12:1–12; Luke 10:29–37 and Luke 15:1–31.

Peter (PEE-ter) was a fisherman. He and his brother, Andrew, were the first two apostles Jesus chose. He was first named Simon, but Jesus changed his name to Cephas, which means 'rock' in Aramaic. In Greek the name is Peter. Peter, James and John were Jesus' closest friends. Peter was the first to tell the Good News of Jesus to the non-Jewish people. Later in his life, Peter wrote the New Testament books of 1 and 2 Peter. He probably died as a martyr for Christ. (Matthew 14:25–33; 16:13–18; Mark 14:27–39; Luke 22:54–62; John 20:1–6; Acts 3:1–26; 10:1–48)

PETER

Pharisees (FA-rih-seez) means 'the separate people.' They were a Jewish religious group who followed the religious laws and customs very strictly. Jesus often spoke against the Pharisees for their religious teachings and traditions. Many of the Pharisees did not like Jesus because he did not follow all of their rules. (Matthew 5:20; 23:23–36; Mark 7:1–13; Luke 18:9–14)

R

repent (rih-PENT) means being sorry for doing something wrong and not continuing to do that wrong thing. To repent is to 'change your heart and life'. (Matthew 3:2; 4:17; Mark 1:15; Luke 15:7, 10; Acts 2:38; 3:19)

S

shepherd (SHEP-'rd) is a person who cares for and protects sheep. A shepherd loves his sheep and gives them food and water. He guides them to a quiet place to rest. He protects the sheep from wolves and other wild animals. A good shepherd will even die trying to protect his sheep.

Jesus is called the Good Shepherd because he loves and cares for his followers who are often called sheep. Jesus was willing to die for his followers to save them. (Mark 6:34; John 10:1–30; 1 Peter 2:25; 5:4)

SHEPHERD

Son of Man was a name Jesus called himself. It showed that he was God's son, but he was also a man. This title for Jesus comes from 'one who looked like a human being' in Daniel 7:13–14. There Daniel prophesies about Jesus. (Matthew 24:30; 26:64; Mark 13:26; 14:62; Luke 21:27; 22:69)

T

temple (TEM-p'l) is a building where people worship their gods. God told the Jewish people to worship him at the Temple in Jerusalem. This Temple had been built by King Solomon. It was later destroyed by the Babylonians. It was rebuilt by Zerubbabel. This Temple was destroyed by a Roman general, Pompey. Herod built a third Temple which was used in Jesus' time. (Mark 11:15–17; Acts 7:47; 19:27)

Thaddaeus (THAD-ee-us) was one of the 12 apostles. Little else is known about him. (Matthew 10:3; Mark 3:18)

U

unleavened bread (un-LEV-'nd bred) is bread made without yeast. This kind of bread is like a flat, thin cracker because it does not rise when it is baked. God told the Jews to use unleavened bread for the Passover Feast. (Matthew 26:17–29; Mark 14:12–25)

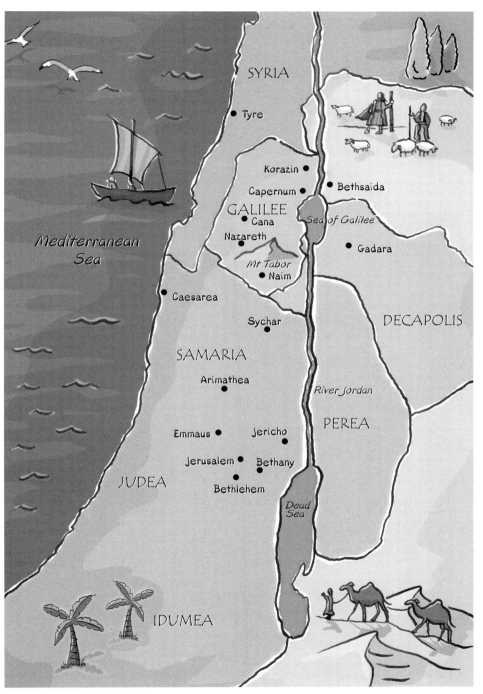

The Holy Land in the Life of Jesus

INTERNATIONAL CHILDREN'S BIBLE

My child, pay attention to my words.
Listen closely to what I say.
Don't ever forget my words.
Keep them within your heart.
These words are the secret to life
for those who find them.

THE GREATEST COMMANDMENT

"'Love the Lord your God with all your heart, soul and mind'. This is the first and most important command. And the second command is like the first: 'Love your neighbour as you love yourself'. All the law and the writings of the prophets depend on these two commands."

NOTES

Do you want to read more of the Bible?

Then get the full edition of The International Children's Bible

HB: 9780850099010

HB: 9781860244315

The *International Children's Bible* is not an adult Bible especially packaged for children. It has specifically been translated directly from the Hebrew and Greek texts into English so that it can be read and understood by children between the ages of 6 and 12.

The *ICB* is a full text Bible that every child will be delighted to own. With guidance, daily Bible reading can easily become a pleasurable habit that will last a lifetime.

Features of the full *ICB* include:
• Large, easy to read type in two columns
• Simple footnotes explain names, customs and phrases
• 32 full colour illustrations with multicultural images
• A dictionary helps explains difficult words and phrases
• Presentation page
• Colour maps
• Ribbon marker

With simpler language and extra notes and helps, the *ICB* is the perfect Bible for a child who is ready to move on from a picture Bible to a full text Bible.

Hang out with the disciples and find out

what Jesus' story is all about!

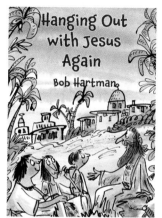

PB: 9781788930291   PB: 9781788931199

Big Bart, Tommo and me, Pip. Three guys on a three-year adventure, hanging out with Jesus, finding out what he's up to. Not exactly the best known of the twelve disciples, but we're on the edge of the action – out of the limelight, where there is plenty of partying, messing about and time to make idiots of ourselves.

We're best mates. And Jesus' mates, too. Every day with Jesus is so special, I've written the stories down; stories you'll find in the Bible if you take a look. Well, sort of, because everything is just a little bit different when you're hanging out with us.

Authentic

We trust you enjoyed reading this book
from Authentic. If you want to be
informed of any new titles from this author
and other releases you can sign up to the
Authentic newsletter by scanning below:

Online:
authenticmedia.co.uk

Follow us: